WHEN THE WORLD CLOSED

A magical adventure to inspire social
and emotional growth during isolation

STORY BY
E.E. Thorgaard

ART BY
J. Shapiro

When the World Closed empowers children to navigate their feelings and reignite their imaginations during the coronavirus pandemic shutdowns.

Educators, Parents, Mental Health Counselors, Psychologists, and Literacy Specialists agree that this dynamic author-illustrator team captures the present times with the emotional depth and hope that children need and deserve.

Parents, educators, and caregivers are encouraged to use this story as a starting point for positive conversations with their children about the difficulties they are facing during these unprecedented times.

Special thanks to our early readers and advisors for their thoughtful contributions including Anna, Annie, Catherine, David, Don, Glenn, Jeffrey, Jess, Jodi-Tatiana, John, Kelsey, Kirsten, Lauren, Maura, Meg, Nancy, Nick, Sarah, Shrreya, Taher, and Yingzhao.

First paperback edition November 2020

Book design by J. Shapiro

ISBN 978-1-7361859-0-2 (hardcover)
ISBN 978-1-7361859-1-9 (paperback)

Whentheworldclosed.com

For my David, thank you for the magic of dreams;
for my Parents, thank you for roots and wings;
and for my nieces and nephews, thank you for all of your colors;
with so much love and so many thanks.
-E

May this story inspire my nieces to use their creativity and
imaginations to make magic of the mundane - thank you for
inspiring the children in this story. This book is for Jeffrey and
my family, my biggest fans and strongest foundations.
-J

For a while, it has seemed just *impossible* to have fun.

It started out okay when Mom said I wasn't going to school one day.

I wondered if it was a snow day – that would be exciting!

I looked out the window, but there was no snow.

On snow days, we usually get to *relax*.

For me, relaxing often means reading
lots of books.

I love to relax!

Other snow days, we walk to Great Grandma's house!
She's 105 years old and lives in a special home.

Sometimes I wonder what she does all day, stuck in her room with nowhere to go.

I didn't know *what* I would do if *I* was stuck with nowhere to go for so long.

That particular snowless day, we went to the grocery store.
But the store felt different. It felt *weird*.

As we shopped, I noticed that lots of things
were missing from the shelves. One aisle
had nothing in it at all! Mom hurried us
along to the next aisle.

OUT OF STOCK

It felt like we were in a *rush*.

The next day, I asked Mom why I still couldn't go to school. Mom paused before answering, "Well, some people at your school were sick. So they had to close it to make sure no one else would get sick."

Was Teacher sick? Were my friends sick? I had a *lot* of swirling thoughts and questions.

That day, Mom couldn't play with Tate and me like she usually did when she was home with us. She had to *work*.

Mom didn't usually *work* at *home*. She said my new job was to keep Tate from interrupting her.

Days and days, or weeks and weeks, or months and months went by like that. I lost track.

At some point, Mom made an announcement. "Finley, you get to start working at home too!"

I wasn't sure how I felt about this. I hadn't seen Teacher in like *forever*. What if he didn't remember me? What if I didn't remember the things he had taught us before school closed?

I didn't like having school without *going* to school.
I wanted someone's help in *real life*. Mom couldn't
help because she was working too.

While we were busy, Tate kept breaking things and
making messes – that was no help. I knew Tate
really wanted to play, but Mom and I couldn't play.
We had to *work*.

Eventually, I was sick of working.

I wanted to go to the park.
I wanted to go see my friends.
I wanted to go *somewhere*.

We always used to *go, go, go;*
but now all we did was *stay, stay, stay.*

I started to wonder. *I* wasn't sick,
so why couldn't *I* leave the house? I
know that when someone is sick they
should stay home, but why should *I*
stay home if *I'm* not sick?

As soon as I had that thought my stomach started hurting. My skin felt hot. I felt a tickle in my throat. Maybe I *was* sick.

Mom took my temperature and it was normal. "You're worried," she told me, "but you're not *sick*." That made me feel better for a moment.

I started wishing I could go far, far away.

To cheer me up, we called Great Grandma.

I told her all the things I was upset about. I wished I could go be with her instead of just seeing her face on a screen.

Great Grandma said that the safest place to be *was* home. "But," she added with a twinkle, "walls don't trap us," and she suggested I build a blanket fort.

So, the next day, I did just that. Tate stopped pouting in the corner long enough to come help me. Soon we were making something cool!

We made a floor of pillows, walls of chairs, and a roof of blankets and brooms. We used boxes, cushions, and flashlights. By the time we were done, the fort was *magical*.

Inside the fort, we told stories, made up songs, smiled, and laughed. We rhymed every word we could with "Abracadabra!" *Shmabracadabra! Labracadabra! Babracadabra!*

Mom brought a snack inside and ate with us. When she left, she forgot the food tray, so I popped out the door to bring it back to her.

Outside the fort was so bright I was nearly blinded!

I've heard that I should believe things when I *see* them, but I couldn't believe my *eyes*!

"Tate! Come quick!" I squealed frozen in place.

"Tate, I have a feeling we're not in our living room anymore," I gulped.

The world outside our fort *sparkled*.

To our right was the biggest Ferris wheel I had ever seen!

We stood below light posts that sparkled all around us.

We looked back and forth from where we stood to our fort.

We wondered what would happen if we went back inside...

Back in our fort, we quickly turned around and peered out. We were blinded again by golden light!

For a moment it was quiet, and then suddenly sirens and flashing lights zoomed in circles around us. The noise was so surprising that we slammed our blanket doors!

We looked quickly at each other and then burst out laughing!

Once we opened our blanket doors again, we wandered through a park lined with trees. The trees were flat on top - I wondered how that could be!

All of a sudden, we came upon a huge metal tower!

"Bonjour," a child said to us with a wave!
We started walking closer, but he put up his hand.
"My Pépé says we must stay at least two meters apart," he said.
"Is that because you are sick?" I asked him.
He shook his head, "It is to protect each other in case one of us is
sick and doesn't know it, just like this mask I'm wearing."

All of a sudden, I felt bad that we weren't wearing masks too.
What if we were sick and didn't know it? What if we got *him* sick?

I wondered how you could be sick and not *know* it.

"Au revoir," the boy said as he zoomed away after a cat.

We walked back to our fort, leaving behind the flat trees, and the tower, and the boy with the mask. When we opened our blanket doors again, we were *ready*.

The voices of people singing surrounded us as we left our fort. We looked up and saw someone in each window playing a different instrument. Somehow, stuck in their houses alone, they were all still making music *together*!

We danced down the streets to the spirited sounds.

As they sang, we played hopscotch with the squares on the ground. We jumped between small squares and big triangles, from grey ones to brown ones, to white ones. We laughed with the pigeons as they played hopscotch with us!

Eventually a pigeon chased us all the way back into our fort!

We rolled on our pillows, laughing until our bellies ached.

As soon as we caught our breath, Tate bulldozed back through the fort doors.

Our jaws dropped in wonder at a castle made of candy! We shivered with a gust of wind.

As we walked, I remembered the boy's Pépé: we stayed far apart from other people walking by and kept our shirts pulled up over our faces.

Eventually, the chill of the air encouraged us back into our fort, where we warmed up.

When we stepped outside again, we were greeted warmly by an older girl.

She asked us how we appeared there. I shrugged in response, and we laughed at how silly it all seemed.

Tate swayed with the wind as butterflies fluttered around us.

We imagined reaching the top of the nearby tower on the back of the farthest butterfly.

Eventually, we pretended to fly on our butterfly back into our fort.

Next, warm breezes fluttered open our door.

Set apart from the darkened sky, bright colors and soft lights filled our eyes.

A child younger than Tate skipped over to us. "Hailo," she said brightly. You could tell she smiled with her eyes. She went to remove her mask when an older girl stopped her and moved her quickly away. I remembered the boy's Pépé and knew that was for the best.

As I looked out over the next amazing place we landed, I was surprised to feel *calm*.

Each place we had seen was different. Each person we saw was special. But somehow they were also *the same*.

The people we met were a little afraid, trying to stay safe. They were also a little lonely, wanting to be together; just like me, and just like Tate.

When we left our fort again, the dark night was filled with light!

We sat still, blocked from walking down the street, but *amazed* by what rose above us.

Before we knew it, we were back in our fort, listening to loud, bounding thumps.

We peaked back out our doors and saw animals taller than Mom jumping over our fort!

Tate ran around the beach after the creatures. I sat very still in the sand as their towering parents sniffed me.

They must have decided I was okay, because we sat together for a while watching the waves roll in and out while Tate played.

Back in our fort, my stomach dropped. For the first time, I realized I had no idea how to get home!

We slowly opened our fort doors once again and stepped out.

"Ni hao," a small boy greeted us. We noticed the people moving around nearby.

"How is it that so many people are able to be outside here?" I asked the boy. He smiled and said warmly, "We weren't allowed to for a long time. I couldn't go to school, or visit my cousins. But now, Ba says it is becoming safe again."

For some reason, hearing that made me feel less *heavy*.

We watched the world hurry by for a while
before it was time to go back into our fort.

Tate smiled, and curled up under my arm as we
laid down on our pillow floor.

I, too, let myself slowly blink off the lights.

We woke up to Mom coming into our fort. "Great Grandma wants to talk to you," she announced!

She brought Great Grandma's video over to us. We started telling her about all of our adventures. Mom laughed at our *wild* stories.

Great Grandma didn't say anything at all, but her eyes *sparkled* at us.

I'm not sure why, but since that day, I have felt less alone.

I see now that the whole world is trying to stay safe. And that while the world is closed, we are all home alone, *together*.

THE END

A NOTE FROM THE AUTHOR

When the World Closed was written to help children navigate their feelings and reignite their imaginations during the 2020 novel coronavirus pandemic shutdowns. This time of change and uncertainty has been challenging for many of us, including the youngest among us. We worked hard to capture some of those challenges with the age-appropriate emotional depth that children need and deserve. It is important to note, however, that each unique experience of the pandemic has been different, and that while we are all facing this together as a human community, we are also seeing things through our own eyes. We encourage you to consider which parts of the story are true for you, and which may be different from your personal experience.

There is no right age for the children who we hope will enjoy and learn from this book. However, it was written for children who have begun reading themselves, likely around 5-9 years old. With that said, every child is different and has different reading needs, so please consider your own knowledge of your children in how you approach this story with them. Some children may want the story read aloud to them while others may want to read it themselves. Either way, we encourage you to talk with your children about the book if you can.

For some children, this book may even be best split across two days of reading time. For them, we recommend leaving a bit of a cliffhanger for the second day by breaking up the book at the point in the story where the characters are just realizing the magic of their fort, right after the words, "The world outside our fort sparkled."

Parents, educators, and caregivers are encouraged to use this book as a starting point for positive and open conversations with their children about the difficulties they may be facing during these unprecedented times, as a way to heal together. As such, we suggest several points of discussion that may be helpful places to start, being sure to define any words that your children may not know, and encouraging children to only share that which they feel ready to share:

Recommended topics and questions for discussion:

For the first half of the book, before traveling the world:
- How do you think Finley and Tate felt at the beginning of the story? How did those feelings change?
- Have *you* felt any of the feelings Finley or Tate felt throughout the story?
- Have you felt any *different* feelings from Finley or Tate throughout the pandemic?
- Have any of the things that changed in Finley and Tate's lives during the pandemic also changed in your life?
- What other things have changed in your life during the pandemic that aren't in the story?
- How do these changes you have experienced recently make you feel?
- Do you hope that any of the changes will stay after the pandemic is over?
- Why do you think Mom wasn't wearing a mask in the grocery store at the very beginning of the story?

For the second half of the book, after traveling the world:
- Why do you think Great Grandma suggested that Finley and Tate build a blanket fort?
- How does it make you feel to know that most of the world is going through similar things at the same time?
- Do you know anyone who is experiencing the pandemic differently than you are?

- Have you ever seen any of the places in the story before in real life? What are those places like?
- Which places that you haven't seen before in real life would you most like to see? Why?
- Can you find any of the places in the book on a map or globe?

The places in the book that Finley and Tate visited are meant to be a very small representation of the places hardest hit by the novel coronavirus (in terms of per capita COVID-19 cases) at the time that the book was written (which is now quite a while ago!). We would have absolutely loved to show even more of the amazing places of the word, but there just weren't enough pages! Here is a hint at where we imagined that some of the scenes in this story might have taken place (in order of appearance): London, England; Madrid, Spain; Paris, France; Milan, Italy; Moscow, Russia; Tehran, Iran; Agra, India; Cape Town, South Africa; Rio de Janeiro, Brazil; Cape Schanck (Victoria), Australia; and Wuhan, China.

We worked hard to make the locations geographically (and even temporally) as accurate as possible. You might have noticed that some of these locations even had pandemic-related imagery on the landmarks (like the COVID-19 particles that were projected on Azadi Tower in Tehran, or the heart and mask projected on Christ the Redeemer in Rio de Janeiro). These were among many places around the world that projected lights on their buildings to raise awareness about the pandemic and show solidarity with patients and essential workers. The many butterflies in our image of Tehran are Painted Lady Butterflies; due to changes in Iran's climate in recent years, these butterflies have been found filling the skies in Tehran more than ever before. While those images are accurate, you might notice that some other images are stretches of our imaginations. For instance, in Paris, you can no longer run around directly under the Eiffel Tower. In Agra, there were likely not people walking around the grounds of the Taj Mahal during shutdowns, as it was closed. In Victoria, you should not jump around the beach with wild Kangaroos. If you were to go to London when this story took place, you would see that Big Ben was really covered in scaffolding. We took creative license with these and other images to keep in the spirit of imagination!

In that same spirit of imagination, we ask you to keep an eye out for some of the other symbolism throughout the story. For example, you may have noticed that most of the people shown throughout the world were children. This was done to keep the perspective of the child as the focus of the story. However, we imagined that their caregivers were close-by and that the children were not off exploring their cities entirely on their own! The exception to this was in China, where there were people in the background. This indicates China's reopening after strict quarantine restrictions were lifted over the course of our writing and illustrating this book. To us, this reopening allows Finley and Tate to feel hope that the pandemic and related shutdowns will eventually end for them as well.

We invite you to read more about this book and other original content about social-emotional learning, child development and mental health, reading best practices, fun ideas for stay-home activities that you can try with your families or classes, and ways to decorate your room with images from this book by visiting our website **whentheworldclosed.com**

We hope you stay safe and healthy, and we thank you for going on this adventure with us!

ABOUT THE AUTHOR

E.E. Thorgaard experienced wanderlust as soon as the 2020 pandemic began! When not video chatting with her 11 nieces and nephews, eating ice cream by a local pond, or playing with her newly adopted puppy, she has been using her knowledge of cognitive psychology and education to write developmentally appropriate books for children and provide resources to their caregivers and educators.

ABOUT THE ILLUSTRATOR

J. Shapiro experiences wanderlust all the time! When not promoting KodiakCare, a non-profit organization that helps families afford life-saving care for their dogs, she has been using her expertise in fine art and graphic design to imagine the unique watercolor technique that created the vibrant landscapes and deep emotions of the world as it is showcased in this book.

Made in the USA
Middletown, DE
21 January 2021

32004150R00031